Tap Into The Power Of The Chant

Attaining Supernatural Abilities Using Mantras

By Baal Kadmon

Copyright information

Kadmon, Baal

Tap Into The Power Of The Chant - Attaining Supernatural Abilities Using Mantras
—1st ed

Printed in the United States of America

Cover image : #80535144 © brizz666 - Fotolia.com
Book Cover Design: Baal Kadmon

Disclaimer

Occult Courses

Over the years, I have received many hundreds of emails asking me if I would ever consider creating online video courses. At first, I was unsure. After so many emails, I decided it was time.

I am now offering courses.

If it interests you in learning more about the **Occult, Meditation, Ancient Languages and History**, you will not be disappointed.

All courses will all be accessible, informative and affordable.

Please go to www.occultcourses.com

There you will find my current courses and all the upcoming courses. If you see a current course you are interested in, you can sign up and get **instant access.**

If you see a future course that interests you, sign up to the mailing list and I will notify you upon its release.

All courses come with a **30-day, no questions asked, money-back guarantee**. If a course is not for you, just let me know, and I will refund you.

Please go to www.occultcourses.com

Introduction

If you have read my other books you know that I recommend the use of mantras as a vehicle for magick. They are very powerful and often times easy to recite. In my other books that deal with mantras I provide a bonus chapter on something called "Siddhi". I have been asked several times to go into greater depth about this and so I have decided to write this text.

By attaining Siddhi, while using a mantra, you are literally embodying the power of that mantra. You will have the mantras power. For example, if you are looking to attract material abundance, the seed mantra for that is SHREEM. If you recite SHREEM 10,000 times, you will attain the essence of that Supernatural power. You will be able to recite SHREEM and attain your material goals easily. You will be a magnet as it were. You will attain supernatural powers. Please note that there are several levels of Siddhi so 10,000 recitations is just the start.

In this book, we will discuss, in greater depth, what Siddhi is. After that, I will present a few powerful mantras and provide you the exact number of recitations you will need to attain Siddhi. Not all mantras have the same recitation count. I will also provide helpful tips on how to keep track of your recitations and most importantly, we will discuss the immense responsibility given you once you achieve Siddhi. Do not take this lightly, once you achieve Siddhi for any given mantra, you will possess that power. USE IT WISELY.

Chapter 1 - Siddhi

Like the Mantras in this book, Siddhi is a Sanskrit word. Its definition describes exactly what it will help you achieve. It means attaining "Perfection, attainment and accomplishment". As stated above, it is often used to describe the attainment of supernatural powers. Often people associate it with Hinduism, but Buddhism also has a rich tradition of Siddhi. In this book, however, we will discuss Hindu mantras in terms of Siddhi attainment.

People who meditate, magicians and other folk who have a supernatural or spiritual practice often seek to attain Siddhi to obtain control over spiritual entities, forces of nature, other people and one's own self. Often, they do not realize they are doing so. For example, many yoga instructors and meditation experts tell people to recite the mantra "OM" in order to attain peace of mind and grounding.

Little do they know that for every recitation they do, they are one step closer to mastering the mantra. It's for this reason the mantra seems to provide great peace to so many people. They have achieved Siddhi and they do not even know it. What's more interesting is that if they knew that they have attained Siddhi, they would then be able to focus the OM energy into supernatural powers. The fact they don't know this might be for the best. I have seen many yoga instructors and casual practitioners of meditation that probably should not know they have just attained supernatural powers. It could get ugly if they knew.

As I mentioned above, many people do not know they have attained Siddhi because they do not realize that Siddhi is a supernatural state of mind as well. Pronouncing the mantras with intention creates a state in the mind that once you use the mantra deliberately, it alters your perception as well. In this sense, if one is aware of this, anyone could attain true Siddhi. But to use it, one needs to be aware of it and like I implied, most do not and should not even attempt to attain it for their own safely and the safety of others.

If you look at not only the Hindu tradition, but in every single spiritual tradition you have stories of ancient and modern accounts of people who have supernatural powers. These powers often are accompanied by mantra recitation or prayer. All these accounts are accounts of Siddhi attainment. Since we will be talking of Siddhi within the Hindu context (Other volumes will discuss other traditions). In the next chapter, we will discuss the various kinds of Siddhi found within Hindu Scripture. After that, I will introduce you to the mantras we will be using and their respective Siddhi recitation thresholds and powers. Then we will discuss the tools you will need and other tips on how to successfully attain Siddhi.

Chapter 2 - Different Categories Of Siddhi Powers In The Hindu Tradition

In this chapter we will discuss the various Siddhi categories mentioned throughout the Hindu traditions. The list below is not mean to be exhaustive, but it does represent the most common power categories. When available, I will call them by their Sanskrit names. Many of these supernatural powers will seem a bit odd to the western mind because they will be taken out of context. Despite this, some of these powers will sound familiar since in many western traditions, Saints, Rabbis, monks, Imams and priests were known to have one or a few of these powers below.

Different types of Supernatural powers obtained through Siddhi:

1. Anima: This ability is to reduce oneself in size, even as small as an atom.

2. Mahima: This ability allows you to grow in size.

3. Garima: This allows you to grow very heavy.

4. Laghima: Levitation (Almost all spiritual traditions speak of people who can do this.)

5. Prapti: This form of Siddhi will allow you to obtain whatever it is you want from anywhere it may be.

6. Ishitva: This is to obtain unlimited power over the entire universe (This might be a bit ambitious for most of us).

7. Vashitva: To control anything you want.

8. Yathā saṅkalpa saṁsiddhiḥ: Achieving anything you desire.

9 Tri-kāla-jñatvam: This category will help you glean Knowledge of the past. present and the future.

10. Para-kāya praveśanam (vikranabhav): The ability to enter another person's body, almost a form of subjugation.

11. Advandvam not being bothered or subjected to dualities of the world such of Hot and cold, pleasure and pain, Sweet and sour, good and evil etc.

12. Para citta ādi abhijñatā: Reading people's minds.

13. Manaḥ-javah (manojvitva): Moving your body wherever you want.

14. Aparājayah: becoming undefeated in anything you do.

15. Dūra-darśanam: Clairvoyance, but also includes seeing things that are very far.

16. Dūra-śravaṇa: Clairaudience, but also includes hearing thing that are very far.

17. Anūrmi-mattvam: Being able to control all cravings of the body and mind.

18. Controlling the weather.

19. Bi-location or being in two places at once.

As you can see, there are quite a few different categories and there are quite a few more. Many of these we will not be dealing with since they aren't as practical as you might think.

In this book we will look to achieve supernatural powers that will help us in the following:

1. Attract Love and sex
2. Attract Material wealth and abundance
3. To master the energy of protection (you can use it whenever you feel threatened)
4. To gain super learning powers
5. To remove all obstacles in your life
6. To conquer your enemies (Please be careful with this one)
7. To Gain Spiritual knowledge as well as psychic power

Although there are thousands upon thousands of mantras we can choose from, we will use only 7 mantras in the class of mantras called "Seed Mantras" Or Bija mantras. They are one-word mantras so gaining Siddhi is much easier to achieve. I will perhaps add more complex mantras in a future volume in this series, but for now these should suffice. Before I go into them, I'd like to discuss why mantras are so important. Some of the text in the next chapter is an extract from my book VASHIKARAN MAGICK - LEARN THE DARK MANTRAS OF SUBJUGATION.

Chapter 3 - Why Are Mantras Important?

When one thinks of Mantras we tend to think of the most famous mantra; OM. OM is, in fact, the primordial mantra; a mantra that the divine used to create the universe. It is no coincidence that many other mantras start with OM. It charges it with power.

The very word Mantra indicates what it is. It is originally in Sanskrit and is comprised of two words. MAN which is the root word for the "MIND" and TRA the root word for "Instrument". It is literally an instrument of the mind. It is said that ancient gurus and sages had the ability to hear the primordial sounds of the universe as well as the root sounds and vibrations of the Gods. They realized these sounds are the very sounds of creation. These very sounds that are at the core of everything, even the divine itself. Modern Quantum physics backs this with the idea of String theory. The theory suggests that the very core of the universe is composed of strings that vibrate a certain frequency. We are not talking atoms but sub, sub , sub atomic...the core of it all. The core vibratory energies of all there is and will ever be.

The original Mantras were composed in Sanskrit. Sanskrit letters contain energetic principles that when pronounced produce changes in the surrounding energy field. The first Mantras ever composed can be found in the Vedas. The Vedas are the most sacred texts of the Hindu faith and some would say the most ancient texts known to man.

The use and function of a mantra as well as their structure varies from tradition to tradition. We often think that Hinduism is one homogenous religion, however, it is incredibly rich and diverse. Probably the most diverse religion in the world. In all traditions, mantras play a role, but some place added importance to them. For example, in the Mysterious Hindu Tantric traditions the Mantra itself contains the very essence of A God or Goddess. Almost as if the Mantra itself was the very name of the deity. So, when they are recited, they immediately invoke the power of that deity. In some schools, Mantras are given specific meaning and are attached to human aspirations such as to gain peace, love and what have you. In other traditions they do not mean anything. But rather their very sound conveys certain energies. Essentially, a Mantra may not have any translatable meaning but rather is used to invoke a certain energy to be experienced.

In this book, we will be dealing with one of these schools of thought; we are using them more for the energy they represent and how to use them to gain supernatural powers. As I stated in the previous chapter, we will be using 7 seed mantras. In the next chapter I will briefly discuss what seed mantras are and then I will discuss each one, their powers and how many recitations are needed to achieve various levels of Siddhi.

Chapter 4 - Seed Mantras

Seed Mantras, also known as Bija or Beej Mantras are root sounds in the Sanskrit language. They are, as their name implies, the root energetic sounds behind the entire universe. These Seed Mantras are the vehicle of power that when used properly, can change the entire vibration of your life.

The Vedic / Sanskrit language in which we find the Seed mantras, is derived from a very ancient language comprised of all the seed mantras. As I stated in the previous chapter, the mantra OM is a single syllable seed or root mantra. Mantras in and of themselves are very powerful and should always be used with respect and with your full attention. I created this book in such a way that it will be easy for you to maintain focus on the mantras.

The Seed mantras that will follow are the core sounds, these sounds have embedded into them the universal creative energies. They are potential power and do not have attributes such as " good and evil". These sounds transcend those human labels. However, it does not mean they cannot be used for both " good and evil". As I stated in other books, the universal energies are like electricity. It will manifest in the way it is guided. Example, plug in your computer and your lamp and you will see they are using the same electricity, but it is manifesting differently in each object based on its intended use. If you stick your tongue in an electric socket you will quickly learn that electricity will light you up as well.

The same when you use these mantras. Mantras do not have morality issues, they are not biased; they are simply energies waiting to be guided and guide them we shall.

In the next chapter. we will go through a description of the seed mantras and their Siddhi "Threshold" for lack of a better term.

Chapter 5 - Seed Mantras And Siddhi

As stated earlier in this book we will look to achieve supernatural powers that will help us in the following aspects:

1. Attract love and sex
2. Attract material wealth and abundance
3. To master the energy of protection (you can use it whenever you feel threatened)
4. To gain super learning powers
5. To remove all obstacles in your life
6. To conquer your enemies (Please be careful with this one)
7. To Gain Spiritual knowledge as well as psychic power

1. Attract Love and sex

The Seed Mantra for this aspect is KLEEM. Pronounced (like Cream, but with a KL instead of CR) This mantra is a very well-known and powerful mantra used to attract love, friendship, peace of mind, sex. If you have a specific intention in mind, chanting Kleem will help you resonate with that intention and manifest it in your life.

How Many Recitations to Achieve Siddhi: 1008 times a day for 21 days (This is a lot easier than you think, you can also chant 10,000 times in one day if you want to hasten the process). This will open just one level of Siddhi. The more you recite the more Siddhi levels you attain.

2. Attract Material Wealth and Abundance

The Seed Mantra for this aspect is Shreem, Pronounced (Shreeem) The Shreem prosperity mantra is a powerful tool that you can use to reshape how you attract and manage your prosperity. Gaining Siddhi in this will be very powerful.

How Many Recitations to Achieve Siddhi: 1000 times a day for 10 days (This is a lot easier than you think, you can also chant 10,000 times in one day if you want to hasten the process). This will open just one level of Siddhi. The more you recite the more Siddhi levels you attain.

3. To master the energy of protection (you can use it whenever you feel threatened)

The Seed Mantra for this aspect is DOOM , Pronounced (DOME) This mantra is generally used for protection. This Mantra is very popular since it is the root mantra for the Goddess Durga in the Hindu tradition. She is the Goddess of Protection. By using this mantra, you are invoking a very powerful protective energy. This mantra is especially good if you want to increase yourself discipline and self- control. Obtaining Siddhi is very beneficial.

How Many Recitations to Achieve Siddhi: 108 times a day for 40 days (This is a lot easier than you think, you can also chant 10,000 times in one day if you want to hasten the process). This will open just one level of Siddhi. The more you recite the more Siddhi levels you attain.

4. To gain super learning powers

The Seed Mantra for this aspect is AIM, Pronounced (AIM, like ready Aim Fire). This Mantra is the seed sound of creativity and intellect and learning. This is a very powerful mantra and can literally change your brain so it opens itself to expanded creativity, enhanced learning ability as well as peace of mind. This is a perfect mantra for students. If you achieve Siddhi you will have super learning and memory abilities. Unlike the others however, this one requires substantially more recitations for Siddhi. But it is worth it.

How Many Recitations to Achieve Siddhi: 10000 times a day for 10 days, or 100,000 times in one day. This will open just one level of Siddhi. The more you recite the more Siddhi levels you attain.

5. To remove all obstacles in your life

The Seed Mantra for this aspect is GAM , pronounced (GUM, like chewing gum) Gum is the seed mantra for the Hindu God Ganesh. He is worshiped throughout India as the God who removes obstacles in life. If you have an obstacle in your life, whether physical or spiritual, reciting this mantra will help clear it away.

How Many Recitations to Achieve Siddhi: 1008 times a day for 30 days, or 10,000 times in one day. This will open just one level of Siddhi. The more you recite the more Siddhi levels you attain.

6. To conquer your enemies (Please be careful with this one)

The Seed Mantra for this aspect is KREEM , Pronounced as Cream) At first, I was hesitant to add this Seed Syllable but I realized this book would not be complete without it. Kreem is associated with a very powerful Goddess in the Hindu tradition by the name of Kali. Kali has been misrepresented in the west as evil, but she is not evil in anyway. She is fierce. Meaning, when you use this mantra you are invoking a fierce energy. If you have a person or people trying to harm you, by obtaining Siddhi, you will develop control over them and they will not be able to harm you. Recite with care, very powerful. **How Many Recitations to Achieve Siddhi: This is a bit different since it requires more a time frame then an actual count. To gain Siddhi, you need to chant this for 30 minutes for 7 days. This will open just one level of Siddhi. The more you recite the more Siddhi levels you attain.**

7. To Gain Spiritual knowledge as well as psychic power

The Seed Mantra for this aspect is OM. Pronounced as OM or AUM, long O) Is the most popular of the Seed Mantras. You may have chanted this yourself at some point in your life, either through a yoga practice or in meditation. Om is the primal sound. By chanting this mantra, you are attuning yourself to spiritual knowledge. This is by far the most powerful seed mantra to obtain Siddhi for.

How Many Recitations to Achieve Siddhi: 125,000 in one sitting or 12,500 a day. This will open just one level of Siddhi. The more you recite the more Siddhi levels you attain.

I know it might seem like a lot, but any powers that you want require you to put in effort. It will be well worth your time. In this next chapter I will give you tips and additional information on how best to perform these chants to achieve Siddhi.

Chapter 6 - Additional Information and Method

In this chapter I will go over briefly how best to approach such mantra chanting for Siddhi.

1. First things first, you should obtain Mala Beads, most come with 108 beads. Each round is one mala cycle. This will help you keep track. You can find the one I use here:

http://www.baalkadmon.com/mala-beads

2. Make sure that you have your intention in mind when you are about to start chanting. If you don't have an intention, these energies can be very dangerous.

3. Although these Seed Mantras are used for specific purposes, you may use them in all areas of your life. They will have a very beneficial influence on you. When you achieve Siddhi, you can use the supernatural power in different ways.

4. You may recite these at any time of the day, I prefer mornings myself.

5. You can record yourself chanting and play it back if you like. I have created Mantra audios that can help you with the recitations. You can find it at

www.baalkadmon.com/mantra-audio-marketplace/

You will want the one that covers the Seed Mantras.

6. These mantras work at the very core. Please approach them with care. If you are not ready for energetic shifts, this practice is not for you. You will gain powers that might be hard for you to control. Please have your intentions clear.

7. You may light incense or candles if you like if you require them. It won't hurt, just be sure to not let them burn unattended.

8. You may recite these mantras silently or out loud. If you are alone, out loud can be very beneficial.

Conclusion

What you have learned here are the very root sounds of the universe. By obtaining Siddhi in them you are harnessing almost "superhero" power. You can do anything with these sounds. These mantras are like electricity, the energy will flow in the direction of the intended output. In saying that please be firm in your intentions and make absolutely sure what you want is truly what you want. Once you achieve Siddhi, you may have those powers for the rest of your life. As they say, be careful what you ask for, you just might get it.

A Note on Mantra Pronunciation

As with most of my mantra magick titles, I have MP3 audios you can purchase if you are interested in learning how to pronounce the mantras in this book. The mantra Audio accompaniment for this book has each of the mantras in this book recited 108 times. These audios are often helpful but are not a requirement.

If you feel you need help with Mantra pronunciations, I have Audios you may find useful. Please go to:

www.baalkadmon.com/mantra-audio-marketplace/

Want To Enhance Your Rituals?

I am not one to promote myself. I like to keep things low-key, but I created a new service that has proven to enhance your rituals and your state of mind and I am very excited about it. As many of you may know, I use Brainwave Entrainment Audios to enhance my writing, my rituals and a lot more. I have been using brainwave products since the 80s. I am using one now as I write this.

I have created hyper-specific Brainwave audios geared to specific spiritual entities. For example, if you call upon the demon, King Paimon, I have a specific audio for him. If you work with the Hindus Goddess Lakshmi, I have a Brainwave Audio for her as well.

Please visit: www.occultmindscapes.com

I am adding Audios every week and will have something for everyone and for every tradition. I am only charging $3.95 per audio MP3 download, with steep discounts for multiple purchases.

1300 have been sold already, I think you will LOVE them.

Other Books By The Author

Organized by date of publication from most recent:

Surya Mantra Magick (Mantra Magick Series Book 13)

Tiamat Unveiled (Mesopotamian Magick Book 3)

Pazuzu Rising (Mesopotamian Magick Book 2)

BAAL: THE LORD OF THE HEAVENS: CALLING DOWN THE GREAT GOD OF CANAAN (CANAANITE MAGICK Book 2)

Chod Practice Demystified: Severing the Ties That Bind (Baal on Buddhism Book 2)

The Talmud: An Occultist Introduction

The Path of the Pendulum: An Unconventional Approach

Durga Mantra Magick: Harnessing The Power of the Divine Protectress

Asherah: The Queen of Heaven (Canaanite Magick Book 1)

Dependent Origination for the Layman (Baal on Buddhism Book 1)

The Watchers And Their Ways

Rabbi Isaac Luria: The Lion of the Kabbalah (Jewish Mystics Book 1)

Circe's Wand: Empowerment, Enchantment, Magick

Ganesha Mantra Magick: Calling Upon the God of New Beginnings

Shiva Mantra Magick: Harnessing The Primordial

Tefillin Magick: Using Tefillin For Magickal Purposes (Jewish Magick Book 1)

Jesus Magick (Bible Magick Book 2)

The Magickal Moment Of Now: The Inner Mind of the Advanced Magician

The Magick Of Lilith: Calling Upon The Great Goddess of The Left Hand Path (Mesopotamian Magick Book 1)

The Magickal Talismans of King Solomon

Mahavidya Mantra Magick: Tap Into the 10 Goddesses of Power

Jinn Magick: How to Bind the Jinn to do Your Bidding

Magick And The Bible: Is Magick Compatible With The Bible? (Bible Magick Book 1)

The Magickal Rites of Prosperity: Using Different Methods To Magickally Manifest Wealth

Lakshmi Mantra Magick: Tap Into The Goddess Lakshmi for Wealth and Abundance In All Areas of Life

Tarot Magick: Harness the Magickal Power of the Tarot

The Quantum Magician: Enhancing Your Magick With A Parallel Life

Tibetan Mantra Magick: Tap Into The Power Of Tibetan Mantras

The 42 Letter Name of God: The Mystical Name Of Manifestation (Sacred Names Book 6)

Tara Mantra Magick: How To Use The Power Of The Goddess Tara

Vedic Magick: Using Ancient Vedic Spells To Attain Wealth

The Daemonic Companion: Creating Daemonic Entities To Do Your Will

Tap Into The Power Of The Chant: Attaining Supernatural Abilities Using Mantras (Supernatural Attainments Series

72 Demons Of The Name: Calling Upon The Great Demons Of The Name (Sacred Names Book 5)

Moldavite Magick: Tap Into The Stone Of Transformation Using Mantras (Crystal Mantra Magick Book 1)

Ouija Board Magick - Archangels Edition: Communicate And Harness The Power Of The Great Archangels

Chakra Mantra Magick: Tap Into The Magick Of Your Chakras (Mantra Magick Series Book 4)

Seed Mantra Magick: Master The Primordial Sounds Of The Universe (Mantra Magick Series Book 3)

The Magick Of Saint Expedite: Tap Into The Truly Miraculous Power Of Saint Expedite (Magick Of The Saints Book 2)

Kali Mantra Magick: Summoning The Dark Powers of Kali Ma (Mantra Magick Series Book 2)

Mary Magick: Calling Forth The Divine Mother For Help (Magick Of The Saints Book 1)

Vashikaran Magick: Learn The Dark Mantras Of Subjugation (Mantra Magick Series Book 1)

The Hidden Names Of Genesis: Tap Into The Hidden Power Of Manifestation (Sacred Names Book 4)

The 99 Names Of Allah: Acquiring the 99 Divine Qualities of God (Sacred Names Book 3)

The 72 Angels Of The Name: Calling On the 72 Angels of God (Sacred Names)

The 72 Names of God: The 72 Keys To Transformation (Sacred Names Book 1)

About Baal Kadmon

Baal Kadmon is an Author, and Occultist based out of New York City. In addition to the Occult, he is a Religious Scholar, Philosopher and a Historian specializing in Ancient History, Late Antiquity and Medieval History. He has studied and speaks Israeli Hebrew · Classical Hebrew · Ugaritic language · Arabic · Judeo-Aramaic · Syriac (language) · Ancient Greek and Classical Latin.

Baal first discovered his occult calling when he was very young. It was only in his teens, when on a trip to the Middle East that he heeded the call. Several teachers and many decades later he felt ready to share what he has learned. His teachings are unconventional to say the least. He includes in-depth history in almost all the books he writes, in addition to rituals. He shatters the beloved and idolatrously held notions most occultists hold dear.

His pared-down approach to magick is refreshing and is very much needed in a field that is mired by self-important magicians who place more importance on pomp and circumstance rather than on magick. What you learn from Baal is straight forward, with no frills. Magick is about bringing about change or a desired result; Magick is a natural birthright…There is no need to complicate it.

www.baalkadmon.com

www.occultmindscapes.com

Follow Him on Facebook and other Social Media Sites:

http://baalkadmon.com/social-media/

Printed in Great Britain
by Amazon